YET MORE FROM
THE FALCONS NEST

YET MORE FROM THE FALCON'S NEST

Bromyard Poetry for Pleasure Group

Yet More From The Falcon's Nest
Compiled by Bryony Cullum, with help from other members,
for the Bromyard Poetry for Pleasure Group

Published by Aspect Design 2022
Malvern, Worcestershire, United Kingdom.

Designed, printed and bound by Aspect Design
89 Newtown Road, Malvern, Worcs. WR14 1PD
United Kingdom
Tel: 01684 561567
E-mail: allan@aspect-design.net
Website: www.aspect-design.net

CONTENTS

SEASONS

CHILDHOOD

FAUNA

HISTORICAL

LOCKDOWN

HUMOUR

NATURE

MISCELLANEOUS

PREFACE

An aim of Bromyard Poetry for Pleasure is to enable poets to meet and share their own poetry. Meeting monthly, at The Falcon Hotel, Bromyard, members bring their poems and ones they think the group will enjoy. Part of the time we will have a speaker or partake of a workshop to extend our learning and abilities.

We were able to keep going during lockdown and found that having poetry in our lives was of benefit. Having Covid and the Platinum Jubilee Celebrations as well as shifting economics we are living in strange times and we thought it was time to share our poems and create a third book. It covers a wide selection of topics, some thought provoking and some rejoicing in our world and local environment. We love to read our members' poems and hope that you will too.

Bromyard Poetry for Pleasure meetings are held on the first Wednesday of each month at The Falcon Hotel, Bromyard, at 11a.m. Anyone can come and just listen or join in. You will be very welcome.

We thank John and the staff of the Falcon Hotel who look after us extremely well.

For further information ring Bryony Cullum 01568 760 558 or bryonycullum@gmail.com

We have a piece in "Off The Record" with details.

PLACE

Home

The home of the eagle is the limitless sky.
This is the highway that migratory birds will fly.
The home of the whale is the rolling sea
Where the dolphin, porpoise and seal swim free.
The home of the ant is the hillock it's made,
A hive of activity, one of nature's wonders that's not man-made.
The home of the robin is the potting shed
Where from a clutch of eggs her family fled.
The home of the rat is under the corn stack.
The rat has no friends the humans see to that.
The home of the squirrel is a cosy little dray.
When the north winds blow and snow lies deep
This little creature is sound asleep.
The home of a child is a special place.
Over the years be it a girl or a boy they will remember
Their home with fondness and joy.
Memories of home where there was laughter and love
And sometimes tears, will travel with them for decades to come.
Now in old age and memories go, the memory of their childhood home
Will come back with a golden glow.

Denis R.H. Teal   October 2021

GIFTS OF THE DOWNS

Today the sun shone
But a sharp wind blew.
Head down, then on the path
A lady bird of scarlet hue.

A tiny beetle shining bronze,
Though dandelions were over,
I saw bird's eye and buttercup
Bluebells and clover.

Above me the new tree leaves
Of ancient oak and beech
Brave ash- I pray for you.
What lessons will you teach?

So much precious life is here,
Insect, birdsong, flower, tree,
Each one a tiny gift
A small surprise for me.

Thalia Gordon Clark

TEME RIVER

A litany of loveliness
The names that grace the twisting Teme.
Come climb together from mouth to source,
Twined with paths its twisting gleam.

Past Bransford's bridge, the barn at Leigh,
Soughing wind through Lulsley's trees,
Grating of gears up Ankerdine,
Cropping of grass on Ham Bridge leas.

Through Martley's red rock portal
The accompanying road descends,
Entrance to her vale of enchantments,
High banks and fast-flowing bends

Long, rounded limbs and female forms
Smooth the valley's steep sides,
Under dark dingles of gruesome name,
Where Severn's wild daughter rides.

A Shelsley with a sandstone church,
The other built of travertine,
Clifton above and Stanford athwart
The river on its wandering line.

Mamble - a secret not to tell -
Eastham's wrecked bridge stood here,
Tenbury's annual mistletoe fair
And Clee whose brow shows clear.

Dreaming cows under orchard trees,
Hopyards and fields of ripening wheat:
A surviving mixed farm, unusual now,
Where Hereford, Worcester and Salop meet.

Turning north at Wooferton,
Ashford Bowdler savours fear,
His sister Ashford Carbonel,
Her pretty bridge above the weir.

Ludlow is a fluttering flag,
High on its prosperous hill,
While just above lies Bromfield,
Horse chestnut shading water-mill.

Swinging west through Downton Gorge
Past Burrington's headstones of iron
To the parlour pub at Leintwardine,
Then Bucknell and Brampton Bryan.

Knighton and Knucklas, train into Wales,
Llanfair Waterdine, Mary's church,
Beguiling Beguildy beckons us to
The final village in our search.

Felindre turns its ghostly wheel,
We leave behind its last abode
To climb up bare Cilfaesty hill,
The last we see of house and road.

The dwindling stream we follow to
A fount that's hidden in a fold,
And here we stand and gaze as if
It were the fabled pot of gold.

We ascend to only earth and sky
And leave behind all settlements,
A journey suddenly back through time
To the primordial elements.

Our pilgrimage is now complete
We've traced it to its bubbling spring.
Our presence makes a sacred place
No gifts we've brought, ourselves we bring.

Now bead the names upon a thread
To make a charm to wake a dream,
That litany of lovely names
Found on the peaceful banks of Teme.

Charles Eden

Blue Hydrangeas

The path was dry, dusty
Swirls of sand rising, falling
Covering brown sandaled feet.

Blue hydrangea bushes growing
Both sides of the track
Their blooms reflecting the sky.

Blending with the sea far below
Bouquets of blue hydrangeas
Their heavy heads drooping.

Reaching the downward path...
Glancing back....You were there
Framed by blue hydrangeas.
Lightly touching their blooms
You waved....Then you were gone.

The sea washed my feet.
Sunshine warmed my face
Drifting into sleep on soft white sand.

Dreaming of blue hydrangeas
Stretching towards the horizon
In glorious smudged lines.

Jane Dallow

Blue hydrangeas was written after seeing them on a young man's grave,
vibrant against the freshly dug earth.

Harpers Bazaar

I wish to celebrate Harpers Bazaar
A mixture of junk shop and gallery.
A riotous eccentric assortment
Worth more than an oil sheikh's salary.

I know - don't get carried away - it's a shop
And Lawrence just making a living,
But if you enjoy the oddness of dreams
It's a place that keeps giving and giving.

Need a pith helmet? You're at the right place,
Want to hide? Racks of camouflage suits.
Books for the hills or sledge for the snow,
All the kit for your favourite routes.

Guides and scouts can be uniformed here,
D of E groups try on their huge rucksacks.
O.K. that cannon was never for sale
But we're all on the look-out for knickknacks.

17

I went in this week and I really must say
That the splendid ceremonial dress
Of the Intelligence Corps, green velvet brocade,
Caught my eye. Must go back and say yes.

Don't tell the P.M. or he'll be along,
As his dressing up box is near empty.
Hard hats and bibs, aprons, medical kits
The Bazaar could supply him with plenty.

And so, sad to say, a very farewell
To providers of Malvern Link colour.
You've brightened our lives with countless supplies
We cannot expect such another.

Charles Eden

The Heathery Space

The heathery space between white crofts.
No hedged slopes and fields like the soft south.
Crags, giant clefts and tumbling water burns,
Silvered shadowed lochs edged with slopes of dark peat earth.
A sea leading out to curves and clambering blue islands.

Judy Malet

Mountain Shadorma

Way up high
The rocks and stones grow,
Reaching blue,
Pulling down
Light and life through wet and storm
The green between shines.

Maggie McGladdery

A shadorma is a short poem with syllable pattern 3,5,3,3,7,5

DOMES DE MIAGE, CHAMONIX

Just a night and a day
Thirty odd years ago
The hut was full so we slept outside.
Then out of our bivi bags
And gear up in the dark
Head torches searching the route
And onto the glacier.

An early hours start
Is the only way
To ensure the snow bridges
Across the crevasses
Are solid to bear our weight.
With the rope taut between us
As we grope our way up.
Still dark when we emerge
From the maze of the glacier
And start up the snow slope
For the sharp ridge.

It's my first alpine climb
We're moving cautiously
Which means we've been slow
And the dawn is arriving
As we balance up the knife edge
Bound for the top.

Reach the summit by dawn
The mantra that pushes us along
So that the snow is still solid
When on tired legs we descend.

But it's already soft
On the ridge to the peaks
Of the Domes de Miage.

The north east to our right
Is awash with bright colours
While night remains still
On the glacier we climbed.

Now the shared summit moment
Permits us a pause
But we must not delay.
The descent begins slushy
And soon we are wallowing
Up to our knees then
Taking a slide and a tumble
Beneath the hot sun.

At last we're on rock
The track goes past the refuge
And down to the road and the valley
And its offerings of green for the eye
Food and drink for the body.

Now sitting outside in the light
Still buzzing with what we have done
Only one night and a day
And that half a lifetime away.

But see how the memory has stayed
How such a memory can't fade.

Charles Eden

Belonging

My mind wanders back and forth,
I always wanted to belong,
To feel content in one place.
I seem to always have come and stayed and gone.
I feel a lostness in the widowed sky.
There is a place?
There is a place where I belong?

Judy Malet

Zeinodin Caravanserai

"Caravanserai" – the very word
Conjures an image of magic and romance,
Of weary travellers from half across the globe
Arriving at a place of peace and calm.
Its walls are like a fortress, high and secure,
With rounded towers to keep the world at bay,
The desert flat and featureless runs far away,
Whilst jagged barren mountains line the sky.
But step within; the coolness welcomes you,
The arches overhead offer a warm embrace,
The central courtyard open to the sky,
Says to you "Come and sit, and stay a while".
The cabins and their carpets bid you rest,

The simple palliasse says "Sleep you here".
The stairs invite you up onto the roof
To gaze upon the desert and the hills.
And yet two miracles are still in store.
The first is watching the sun escape the day,
Running away beyond the western hills,
Leaving a trail of blushing peach then gold,
And hills that cast dramatic silhouettes.

A meal brings sustenance and comradeship,
Laughter and stories, jokes shared and selves revealed,
Until the second miracle occurs.
We climb the stairs again onto the roof
And there the bowl of Heaven is overturned,
A thousand stars are scattered in the night,
From side to side stretches the Milky Way,
And we are shown our insignificance,

But in a caring not a threatening way,
As if the stars are reaching down to say
"Fear not, safe in your caravanserai".

So Graham, leave these words in payment for
The book of memories you take with you.
The heavens are brilliant with multitudinous stars,
There is no pollution!

Graham Hamblin

Along the ancient silk routes in Persia there were a number of resting places.
Zeinodin Caravanserai is one of the few remaining.

Bluebell Wood

Bluebells in the bluebell wood
Billowing blue on blue
Cascading toward the trickling brook
With the little bridge across
Blue heaven in the bluebell wood
Blue velvet on the ground.

Be careful where you put your feet in
That sea of blue
The bluebells are so lush and deep
Stretching on and on
You may fade away tout suite
Into blue on blue.

Bluebirds high up in the tree tops
Sing a bluebird song.
The bluebells sweet perfume
Floats up into the air
Perfume from the Gods.

Tread carefully my darling in
Case you disappear where the
Blue, blue sky meets the
Blue on blue in the bluebell wood.

Jane Dallow

Fencote

Toiling up through late December mud
I discovered this remote surviving station
Atop its hill since 1888
Last passengers departed seventy years ago
Yes, three-score years and ten, allotted span.

Long closed of course but lovingly maintained,
Its Signal Box, its Waiting Room and hearth,
Booking Office, churns lined on the platform,
Its innocent holiday posters, Ladies and Gentlemen,
You'd swear you heard the sound of an approaching train.

And here they are, the girls in frocks, the boys in shorts,
Mothers in their crinolines, the men be-whiskered,

As the train exhales and luggage is unloaded,
Then doors are slammed, a green flag waves, a whistle blows
And it all begins its squealing steep descent.

Suddenly I'm back with the old family albums.
Smudgy sepia to begin then black and white,
Look here is my grandmother, Iona Gwynn,
Whom I never met,
Her beauty radiant still, neutralising time,
What a story she would surely tell me.

But sadly unrecorded names of great uncles and aunts
Unsmiling and stiff in their formal clothes and groups
At long forgotten family events.
They were as real as you and I are now,
Properly attentive to the present, their here and now.

So Fencote, I must thank you for the time and place,
To bring to you my own sepia past,
For a meeting on the station platform
Of all the imaged and imagined souls
This my delighted shout of affirmation.

Charles Eden

Discussions are being held to see if a route for walkers, horse riders and
cyclists can be made along the track of the old line from Leominster to
Worcester via Bromyard.

MY HOME

They say, home is where the heart is.
My home is where the hearth is.
Logs burning brightly, casting shadows which dance across the wall,
Golden shapes lie sleeping, bathed in its warmth.
Whiskers twitched, a muffled growl
Dreams of running on the Downs, or maybe a garden prowl.
Yes...home is where my heart is and there by the hearth my two lovely dogs,
Fluffy and golden, so loyal and so fair,
My two Goldies dream as I sit in my chair.

Val Brazier   2021

I just adore dogs and these two bring such pleasure and joy to my life- A
Golden Retriever and a Labrador Retriever cross: both rehomed guide dogs.

PEOPLE

ELIZABETH. OUR QUEEN

70 years of service
Our sovereign to us has given
To do her duty to her peoples
Is to what the Queen has striven.
Today we give thanks and celebrate
Her platinum jubilee
And a lifetime of devotion
By her majesty.
Long may she reign.
And long has it been
For Elizabeth our Queen.
Over seven decades of our history
The monarch's guidance has been seen.
She is the jewel in our nation's crown
A symbol of constancy.
There, for most of us our whole life.
She gave us a British identity
To more than just our island
She reaches out beyond our shores
To a commonwealth of nations.
To them too a unity she ensures
Her face is known across the world
A United Kingdom she represents
She transcends all and any difference.
Her care for all people is immense.
She maintains impartiality.
With her there is no side.
She is the very best of what is British.

The last bit of our nation's pride.
When you sing the National Anthem.
Think of our gracious Queen.
Whole-heartedly sing those words
And give thanks for what they mean.

Robin Wilson   June 2022

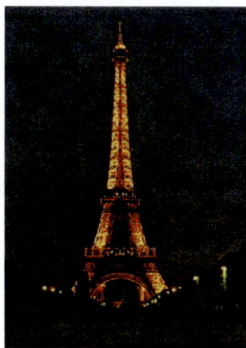

The Man in the White Gucci Shoes

Paris, City of Love.
It's raining in a soft gentle way.
She spots a shop doorway
With a convenient chair.
She sits and watches the world go by.

A young man joins her.
They watch people scurrying past.

He's wearing white Gucci Shoes.
She says "Nice shoes".
He doesn't want to get them wet!

They talk; she tells him why she's there.
Everything comes spilling out.
She bares her soul
To a stranger wearing White Gucci Shoes
In a shop doorway, on a rainy day in Paris,
City of Love.

The rain stops, it's time to go,
To her assignation, her fate,
He says "Alivia, Good Luck." She watches until he's out of sight,
The man in the White Gucci Shoes.

Jane Dallow

A true love story and it had a happy ending.

Philippic

Philippic! I shouted at him.
To stop the torrent of abuse coming from his mouth.
It had the desired effect,
Stopping him in his tracks
The unused word derailing his train of thought.
Such a bitter verbal attack,
In part may be deserved
After my orations against him.

He is beside me, no longer beside himself
With anger, dissipated, as his mind
Seeks to connect to ancient history, long ago studied.
Philippic, I utter, quietly. He smiles, as he
Deftly pulls the word from the recesses of his mind.

Demosthenes, he retorts and retreats,
To Macedonia, perchance?

Ronith Bhunnoo

The Refugees

Walking mile after mile, day after day in the hope that their efforts will
one day pay
And allow them refuge somewhere safe, away from prejudice, violence
and hate.
They carry on walking, wondering their fate
Passing through countries, three whole years it took
A father, his family now about to look towards a future of safety,
They stand on the shore, hoping and praying their lives will hold more
Will their toil be rewarded, will their efforts now pay to provide a safe
future in the longed for U.K?

I saw this as a news report on T.V. The family was huddling inside a
tiny tent, in December, on the French Coast as the father spoke to the
reporters. Quite shocking!

Val Brazier

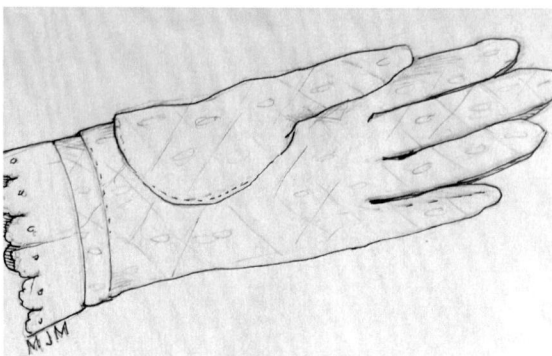

The Glove Makers' Hands

These hands that gripped the cow skin
Torn from flesh that fed the thin.

These hands creating hands, pulled taut
And stitches fine, that ladies bought.

These hands stretched to breaking
Creating rare pieces, while body is aching.

These hands ache for holding
Love's tenderness enfolding

These hands, not gloved or covered,
Not protected as are others.

Can these hands then dream of softness?
Caring- not the drudge of hardness?

My hands, these hands, reach out to feel,
Can the light of hope be real,
That hand in glove, with my love

Entwined, combined,
Fingers griping, no more slipping-
We - can be - secure?

Maggie McGladdery
Written in response to leather gloves made in Ledbury, now in the Butcher's
Row Museum

Alice

Books, essays and endless work to achieve a long held ambition is
the only perk.
Studying hard for exams is now the norm, eyes tired, pencils worn.
Forms filled in just in time, interviews held in person or on line.
No results yet, but hope that all will be fine.
An email arrives, all criteria met for a young girl's dream of becoming
a vet.
My dear granddaughter, Alice, suffice it to say congratulations all
round on such a memorable day.

Val Brazier
Needless to say, I am one very proud Granny.

Christmas Day

Christmas Day
Is always a Sparkling, Sunny time.

Quiet and still, no early morning cars,
Not even on Bluebell Hill.

A present, a kiss, a croissant,
A flurry in a hurry in the kitchen,
A leisurely swim, Xmas biscuits
And a gaggle of giggles,
Then Spirited home.

Replete, for a walk on St. Stephen's Way,
When Janet was at bay.
Later Yasmine would enjoy wrecking the wrapping paper
And her uncle carefully rescued it for next year!

We had Dickens- year after year!

And what now my love?
A Sunny, warm Christmas, perhaps?

Ronith Bhunnoo

Miss Kenard

Miss Kenard's sweet emporium
For children of all ages,
Packed from top to bottom
With glass jars of every description
Filled with sweets of every colour
Reds, pinks, purples, yellows,
Blues, blacks, striped like umbrellas.

Every Saturday I went to see
Miss Kenard for my sweets.
Climbing up steps to the doorway the
Smell of sugar candy, wafting,
Tantalizing taste buds
Bringing pleasure.

Gentle lady with sad eyes,
Rosy complexion like the pink

Sugar mice on the counter
Peeping out of
Sugar paper.

Miss Kenard served her sweets
With quiet reverence, like a
Preacher with a sermon, the
Mice her congregation.
Pear drops, oranges and lemons.
Gob stoppers, three sizes, liquorice sticks ,
Sherbet Dips, Fizz Bombs, Chocolate mice
Tails made from
Sugar and spice.

Crinkly paper bag, rustling
Your sixpence filled it to overflowing
Enough to last a week or a
Day at least.

Generations of children remember
Miss Kenard
Who rarely smiled
Sad Miss Kenard.

Jane Dallow   2011

The Group

As we sit around the table,
Far apart, and very near,
Grasp as firm as you are able
The presence that enfolds us here.

We are friends to one another,
Known and unknown, side by side;
Look and feel towards each other,
Leave alone what we would hide.

Take us now, please, as you find us,
Do not tear the masks away,
For our masks are still part of us
And of the parts we live to play.

Each has facets still in shadow,
Minds and hearts to us unknown;
This is not a cause for sorrow,
If we knew all, we would drown.

A person in entirety
Is an overwhelming thing;
Achieve a small integrity,
Great love is in a little ring.

We are single but together,
Alone but trying to be near;
Dare to be fond with one another,
Love as much as you can bear.

Graham Hamblin

The poem written when the poet was a university student in London.

Absent Friends

Once again the Bromyard Poets gather at this festive time of year
To share their thoughts and dreams over turkey and cold beer.
Some whose work is like a rippling brook in full flow
And others who will raise a smile and a laugh before we go.
The walls of this grand old room of English oak.
Over the centuries must have heard every word ever spoke
On this night of frolics and fun, and food that's fit for a king.
While on our way home on this cold winter's night, we may hear the old church bells ring
After an evening of thought, provoking words, laughter and jest
Let's spare a thought for the words of our absent friends that reside in that old Jacobean chest.

Denis R.H. Teal   December 2012

The old cinema projection room is the "eyrie" of The Falcon Hotel, hence our name for it, The Falcon's Nest. Sylvia provided us with a magnificent Jacobean chest in which to keep our poetry books, some with poems written by members no longer with us.

Touch the screen to start

Touch the screen to start.
The robot gives out her instruction
To touch the screen to start
But unlike the girl at the check-out
A robot ain't got no heart.

I will always choose a person
And not touch the screen to start.
I want to be served by a human
Not told to add to the cart.

The customer in front of me
Is having a bit of a chat
With Steph – he even knows her name
I will not blame him for that.

I don't want Steph to be replaced,
She doesn't just tot up the sums,
She'll chat and try to be pleasant
To whoever for her services comes.

It's the things that help keep us human
That should be top of the list.
It's the robots that are redundant
Rip them out, they will not be missed.

Charles Eden

SEASONS

Tree Dressing

North winds blowing
Winter's icy grip stripping trees
Of their autumn plumage
Leaving naked skeletal branches.

Waiting to be dressed in frosty white
How beautiful they look in
Their sparkling dresses
Clustered close together
Trying to outdo each other.

Snow storms come and go
Covering each tree and branch
With white fur coats.
Bulbs peeping above the ground.

Soft rustling as the earth warms up
Fragrant air brings heady scents of
Pink and white blossom dainty buds of
Palest colours just waiting for the kiss of summer.

When the palette changes to
Greens, reds and yellows,
Burnished copper beeches contrast with the
Birch of pale green and silver.
Autumn the time of the year when jewels appear
Leaves the colour of burnished metals
Treasure to be enjoyed by the wild creatures passing by
Do they stop and wonder at their carpet of many colours?

Black trees against a sullen sky
Waiting for a touch of sparkle
White icing to cover their naked torsos
Diamond icicles, lacy cobwebs without the spiders
Never ending cycle of changes
Dressed to impress as always.

Jane Dallow   2013

Winter

The winter sun struggles.
All the countryside so still,
As if in a deep sleep.

Is it preparing for the
Time of a deep freeze?
Loneliness of its beauty
Echoes in the heart

Music of a life past plays out.
Remembering the winters of the Lakescape
In that place of great beauty.

My heart takes me there
A longing to see once again.

Maybe not in this lifetime.
Feelings so removed.
Was it real?

Rosemarie Powell   2012

Experiencing winter in the U.K. but longingly remembering winter on the
shores of Clark Hill Lake, South Carolina U.S.A.

Is It Spring?

Is it spring?
I see sodden ground;
Grey and cloudy sky day after day.
What do the flowers say?

They say – yellow, yellow
And more yellow.
I see purple, white and yellow.
Yellow- daffodils, celandines,
Dandelions, forsythia.
Aloft I see pink and white.
Spasmodically I did see sky blue.

February fog.
Maelstrom March,
April showers.
A brilliant bright day.
An English spring!

Bryony Cullum   1ˢᵗ April 2020

March

The month of miracles.

The appearance of a tiny rabbit, or the blooming of a fragrant flower
The earth is getting warmer, miracles are being performed every hour.
The gardener with his weathered old hand is tilling the soil bit by bit.
With ancient knowledge he is coaxing the earth its harvest to submit.

With the gentleness of a newborn lamb, silently March comes gliding in
Spring is waiting in the wings and on the 20th of this month enters with
her tin
Of all the colours from nature's store to paint our countryside once more.
Mixed with morning dew she splashes every shade of green replacing the
frosty hoar.

March can be quiet, it can also be loud like an angry lion's roar.
It can bring snow and gales to uproot your trees, blow off your roof and
slam your barn door.
This is the month of sticky buds and pussy willow with a slight breeze
the catkins will dance on the trees.
Now the daffodils, primroses and damson blossom are being courted by
tireless bees.

March is the birth month of my dear old dad, the most wonderful father
a boy ever had.
After fifty years of hard work to retirement he survived, and on his last
day at work
His granddaughter arrived.

March is my month of miracles.

Denis R.H. Teal

SPRING

Daylight lengthens, strengthens,
Percolates, awakens,
Waiting is ending
Fauna and flora begin to flourish,
There is propulsion, an uprising

Spring; a softening
A bounce, resilience, repetition.
A spring sends forth water,
Life-giving,
Refreshing, sparkling ,tinkling.
It expands, spreads, gives bounty.

Spring; a season synonymous with new life,
Exploding, pulsating, developing,
Listen to the birds, the raindrops.
Enthuse in the sunshine.

Take heart.
We have our own personal motivational spring.
Lean on hope. Gather impulses.
Break loose. Spring into action.
Love and enjoy your spring.

Bryony Cullum   February 2021

A Good Life

Bluebells, a carpet of
Scents. The afternoon
Rays of sun, filter
Through the trees
Onto my face
Washing away, infusing
The day, the body, the spirit
With gladness and warmth
And light. A good life.

Ronith Bhunnoo

Hidden Colours

The brownness of winter soils.
The shortness of winter grass.
The shyness of spring bulbs
Slowly they peep out through the grass.
The careful plantings in pots of rich soil
Begin to rise up with handsome leaves,
The white of snowdrops,
The yellow of daffodils.
Our eyes leave the winter colours
And warm in the spring rising.

Judy Malet

Harvest Moon

Harvest moon is out tonight
Shimmering over apple orchards
Where gentle breezes blow
So sweet from the wild rambling rose and
Honeysuckle growing in lush hedgerows.

Vibrant green landscape down narrow lanes
Where the church nestles
In a wooded glade.
Birds sing all day long
The beauty of their song
Lifts the hearts of everyone.

The fields are blessed
By sun and rain and
The red poppy grows
Amongst the golden grain.
Through heady summer days the
Harvests gathered in and when
Autumn starts to bite with
Misty mornings and rainy nights.

The sound of tractors
From dawn to dusk
Gathering in what's left are
Background music to the doves
Cooing to one another about love.
The harvest mouse hurries by
Looking for a place to hide.

Glowing orange in the sky the
Harvest moon shines down and
The autumnal equinox begins. The
Days shorten, winter wins and
The eternal dance goes on.

Jane Dallow   October 2017

A Momentary Glimpse

The leaves are off.
Trees now
Show species tracery by silhouettes
Stark against brightness and cloud.
Distant landscapes are revealed,
Hidden during summer.
Raindrops pattern the window pane
A breeze causes waves on a bush.
The ground is kaleidoscoped with leaves
Resting on perennial green.
A glimpse of colder seasons.

Bryony Cullum   October 2021

Nations Unite

The Vernal Equinox

The Christmas moon was shining bright, as it rolled over
Bromyard Downs on that last November night.
Our market town was calm and serene; the Christmas lights were
the best they had ever been
The shop-keepers dressed their windows with the greatest skill
Giving locals, visitors and children a wonderland thrill.
The tree in the square in all its glory, the star on top telling the
Christmas story.
The spectators were strolling in ones and twos
Praising the team
that had wiped away their winter blues.
Their work is the envy of towns near and far
The Light Brigade always willing to higher the bar.
It's amazing to think that with hundreds of lights and a bauble
It can make life seem almost normal.

The Summer Solstice

The footpath in our market street is widened in case a friend we
normally meet
May shake us by the hand or give us a friendly hug, but in our ear
or up our nose
We may be harbouring this invisible bug so two arms length
between us we must observe
If the regulations we are to serve it was in the Vernal Equinox
when this epidemic arrived
When some of our basic freedoms we were deprived, all through
the summer solstice.

We queued outside the chemist and also for our bread, and
through the radio
We were informed the daily number of dead.

We are now in the winter solstice

We still queue in the street
In the hail, rain ,snow and sleet, for the post office, chemist
and the bakers of our daily bread.
The radio is still telling us to stay at home as it issues the
number of dead.
The vaccine is on route but not proven beyond all doubt
We only hope and pray that in a not too far distant day
The magic potion will force this virus to surrender.
We must all live in hope and with hot water
And carbolic soap
We will beat this horrible thing
And the daffodils will bloom in the spring.

Denis R.H. Teal   December 2020

Cheers to the Spirit

Nature, its leaves have shed
Its vibrancy is dropped
Given up it has
To sleep, retreated
To the inevitable it has yielded

Long cold dark night
Of winter without light
Gloom and doom prevail.

Ah!
Do not despair
Christmas is here!
The festive season it signals
To our hearts it cheers.

Everywhere is ablaze with light.
Every house is illuminated with Xmas light
Breaking the darkness of the night
It's elevation to our spirit

No silent nights
But late nights
Everyone everywhere in party mood
Plenty of parties, drinks and food,
To enhance the festive mood.

Presents adorning Christmas trees
Are shared with friends and loved ones,

No one is left behind
Everyone is so kind.
People, even strangers
Become well wishers.
Thus spreading cheers
And banning the winter blues.

Val Brazier

CHILDHOOD

Childhood

Grandpa's house in the town of soot,
The place where my mother was raised,
Everything black, houses, gardens and cloth.
Net curtains containing the blaze
That was family, the range and the cold outside nettie.

We lived by the seaside, clean air and fine views.
My books and dolls clean and tidy, action ready,
As we read, played, created the next big adventure.
Always encouraged to look after these treasures.
So it really seems strange that the books I was given
At Grandma and Grandpa's small house in the town
Were grimy and dirty, thick pages with pictures
Of far away children and strange sounding names.

Now, my bookshelf of treasures from many years' harvest
Bunnykins, Enid, the great Bunty Annual,
Roald Dahl from the teaching years
Anne Fine and Steve Smallman
Still clean and well cared for but resting alongside
The sooty thick pages my mother kept, I kept
Because memory is not always clean and correct.

Maggie McGladdery

Story for Yasmine from Auntie

Little Ms Parrot
Sat on a Carrot
And the Carrot said "Ow"!
And Ms Parrot said "Wow"!
I didn't know carrots could talk.
And the Carrot said
"You took my seat and
I've sprung a leak.
You're not as light as a feather!"

Part 2

So little Ms Parrot
And her friend the Carrot
Went on a holiday to Slough
Where they said "Wow!
This is great."
And Ms Parrot said
"Wait,
I want to buy a stick of rock."
But the Carrot took a knock
And was grated.
And she said "Wow,
That's not how I like my carrots."
And the Carrot said "Ow,
That's not how I want to be painted!"
And the Painter said
"OK, I'll take a photo

Of how you ought to be."
And he painted the Carrot whole.
And Ms Parrot said to a passing Mole
"Where shall I buy a stick of rock?"
And the Mole said "WHAT?"
And Ms Parrot said "Oh dear!"
And took her friend the carrot back home.

Part 3

I wonder whether
We could fly away?

THE END

Ronith Bhunnoo   2019

Memories of childhood

No water closet there.
First memory,
A potty chair.

One day I found the kitchen cupboard ajar.
Inside an open tin, fingers in.
Contents creamy and white.
Oh, so sweet!

Mother finds me there,
The sticky stuff on my face and in my hair.

Woods and fields surround.
Our ready-made playground.

Runts of the litter brought home by Dad.
Kept warm and fed by Mother.
When big enough to the sty they would go.
A few years passed before I knew
What happened when they grew.

Dad brought home this terrier dog
And tied him to the table leg.
"Do not untie yet" said Dad.
As soon as Dad was out of sight, I let him loose.
Chasing the pup through the house,
Squeals of laughter hit the rafters.
Dad came in, dog ran out, never to be seen again.

Another dog I named Bob.
A faithful companion she became, even though
I gave her a boy's name.
Seventeen years she stayed.

One day from beneath Dad's coat,
A furry bundle, half dead.
Found him in the wood Dad said.

Mother's nursing skills again brought to life
That bundle of red fur.
I called him Reynard.

I took Reynard to my bed and there
He slept till he was grown.
His earthy smell made my sister moan.
One day Reynard got in Dad's bed and bit his toe.
Out of the house Reynard had to go

An old food bin was found and that's
Where Reynard slept, safe and sound.

Reynard became a legend.
The town folk got to hear about this wild thing
And none of us having no fear.
On Sunday afternoons along the lane they would walk.
Stopping at our gate to talk.
How proud my sister and I,
As we showed them Reynard as they passed by.

Reynard left one day.
Dad said it was only right now he had grown
To find those of his own.

Rosemarie Powell   2017

A country childhood in the 1950s.

Grandchildren

I sympathise now with my mother's desire
To have a married daughter and grandchildren.
All conversation with friends and contemporaries
Seemed family centred.
One felt abandoned, excluded,out of the group.

I was never a baby cooer, indeed had rarely handled a baby
Until like one friend
Eventually we breathed a sigh of relief
We'd become pregnant.

Out came the favourites, saved from childhood,
Books, toys animals,
In their turn to be stored again
In hope for future generations.

A friend has accumulated sixteen grandchildren
And maybe more to come. But for some that day does not come,
Again you are outside the circle.
More commonly these days.

The excitement of births, of milestones,of visits;
Maybe you do get tired and are glad to hand them back.
You have become attached to these youngsters.

Sometimes there's a rift.
Those precious contacts lost.
Who can help but marvel
At those fascinating beings,
Grandchildren?

Bryony Cullum   March 2022

The Boogaloo Bird

The Boogaloo bird–
I think I have heard–
Has a wing span as big as a bus.
You may say that's absurd
But the Boogaloo bird
Could not care less about you or us!

He wears yellow boots
As he hollers and hoots
In a nest made of lego and cheese
Which is down in the roots
Of a tree, but it suits
The Boogaloo bird and the bees.

The bees and the bird–
Or so I have heard–
Love to make Lego houses and cars
Whilst eating cheese curd
Which is toasted and stirred
In a pot made of jelly and stars.

The Boogaloo bird–
I'm sure I have heard–
Has a wing span as big as a bus.
You may say that's absurd,
But the Boogaloo bird
Could not care less about you or us!!

Maggie McGladdery

A Father's Gift

Beneath the faded coat
A creature so small,
With fur the colour of its native earth.

The creature would become
Companion, protector of the child
With speckled nose, skin pale as the moon in a shadowy sky.
Eyes the glint of spring leaves.

Bending low he whispers in the child's ear,
"A baby now but soon will grow."
Into my life came the orphan creature.

Rosemarie Powell

Grandchildren

Noses pressed against a cold window, staring out through the glass
The moon and a myriad of twinkling stars in the sky, illuminating the
frost crystals on the grass.
Hoping that when they wake up tomorrow they will see what they
wished for during the night:
A garden carpeted in a layer of sparkling white. They sleep, get up ,
look out, is there snow? Once again due to global warming-no!

They hope each winter for snow, but to date few experiences!

Val Brazier

Adventure

Regarding children's personal growth
An outdoor centre for a week
Is worth a year-maybe much more-
Of normal classroom work.

The residential experience where
You live and eat together
In carefully assorted activity groups
To break down school-induced barriers.

And then the range of challenges
With their different kinds of demand:
Cave, cliff, mountain, river, the sea.
You'll find at least one of them hard.

Amongst the most telling memories
On the knife-edge, a girl, so slight,
Reassuring a strapping youth
Who was gripped and frozen with fright.

And a first taste of sea canoeing,
Paddling through a colony of seals
And- what! The arc of bottle –nosed dolphins,
Was that a dream or was it real?

In utter dark exploring caves,
Sounds, colours and scents forsaken.
And now the relief rediscovering our world
As we emerge and senses re-awaken.

Then the mumbling line flogging up the slope
And the wait for the panting last person
But the widening view high above the vale
And the joy of the shared summit moment.

Sometimes a vista shows nothing man-made
Just ourselves and primeval nature,
Time itself briefly set on one side
For a taste of being immortal.

Then round the meal table that evening
Excited young voices tell their tale
And no one has the time to feel homesick
Experiences that will never go stale.

Inspired by events and the landscape
Some seek expression in music and art
For others it's opened a window
For memories feeding the heart.

Returning just a week later.
Fully exercised mind, body, soul,
And friendships with previous strangers,
Scattered fragments now become whole.

Charles Eden

FAUNA

Thomasina
A Day in the Life of.....

Black furry velvet
Leaping from Mr Smith's sunny window ledge, resting briefly atop
Partridge's hedge
Black furry velvet
Gleaming on old Ms Helen's porch, padding softly into the great hall
of the
Porchester Grand.
Stealthily winding around the spiralling back stairs,
Coiling and recoiling at the vibrations of human pairs.
Swiftly racing the feline mile
In service corridors, deft and adept at invisibly reaching the kitchen,
Invincible in "catching" the fish of the day.

And sated, curiosity increases the fate, the fatality, of the cat.

Bounding upstairs, winding sleek body around door jambs, more
reptilian than feline,
Hitching a sneaky lift in the executive elevator, discreetly stroked by
Miss Levy,
Purring appreciatively at her light touch on ever alert ears.
Reaching the executive floor,
BANG!
Bounding with force straight into the legs of.....The Bouncer? In a
posh 5★ Hotel?
Legs of steel, can't get through, fingers of steel holding me in a vice
like grip around my tum.
Squeezing.
One life gone.

Thrown out of the back door,
Landing with a thud in the wheelie bin, trying to crawl up and out
towards the light,
The lid shuts tight. Not enough air .....
Sleep comes.

So much NOISE!
Banging.
Rattling.
Shouting.
I'm moving! But not on my legs.
I'm being whirled around, banging my head on metal,
Tangling my legs in Sainsbury bags,
Matting my hair in yesterday's foodie remains,
I'm falling, I'm flying!
I'm doing an emergency landing!
Splat.

Crawl, Crawl, on belly flat.
Scrape, scrape, on tarmac, undercarriage ripped.

Rest on soft lawn, old Ms Helen's,
Dream of supping milk, a gentle touch of ear...sleep comes.

Ronith Bhunnoo   2016

Shrapnel
The evacuee cat

In the year nineteen hundred and forty three
Shrapnel the cat became an evacuee.
He came with a family from Liverpool by the sea
To a big house that owned a dog named Ratter
Who turned out to be a right horrible snapper.
The dog liked the mum and the kids
But a Liverpool cat that looked like a rat
This was certainly not for him.

So Shrapnel was billeted in a grocery shop in town;
The highest class grocer for miles around.
This cat from Liverpool by the sea
Thought this is a good home,
It will really do for me.
He had a new cat tray and a china dish for his tea.
He had liver and ham, sausage and spam
Rationing for him was just a sham.

But he needed an observation post
So he could see the clientele that was visiting his kindly host.
He found a space that was an ideal place,
Where he could watch the world go by.
So among the pig's trotters and ham, the butter and spam
Of course the window was the place to be.

So every morning was placed a little white mat
For Shrapnel the evacuee cat.
From here he could watch folk going up and down
With pony and traps carrying farmers in caps
And posh people coming from miles around
In winter and summer, raining or snowing
All getting their rations from
A and E Owen.

Denis R.H. Teal

Jack Russell

Jack Russell in a deck chair,
Looks comfy doesn't he?
He's dreaming of the future
And where he'd like to be.

On a sandy beach somewhere,
Running like the wind,
Doing some retrieving of bouncy balls and things.

Or curled up by a fire
Somewhere nice and hot,
Or right there by the Aga
A warm and cosy spot.

But I know Mr. Russell
You'd like to be with me,
You're dreaming of the ultimate
Cuddle on my knee.

Kate Warren   2011

Betrayal

Friends I've had, friends I'll have, but the one I'll not forget
Was a little dog called Ricky whose coat was as black as jet.
Her eyes were sad and her teeth were worn
We had her from a pet shop soon after she was born.
To us she came so fond and dear
Wherever we were you would find her quite near
With her eyes and her actions to us she would talk.
Through fields and forest with us she would walk.
Joy she would show at our footsteps sound
Until the day I let her down.
The memory still haunts me both day and night
Whenever I recall that pitiful sight,
My friend with trust in her eye and me trying hard not to cry.
I left her in the vet's operating theatre
Knowing full well never more would I see her.
She died.
My friend; she died.
If they allow dogs in heaven, and somehow I know they do,
Then I'll meet again, my friend, so faithful and so true.

Denis R.H. Teal   1971

DOGS

Hard stares and expectant looks as I sit and read amongst my books.
A tail wags, an affectionate lick in the hope I might relent, take a walk,
throw a stick.
They venture outside, highlight of the day for a dog, how could I
remain seated and not go for a jog?

Val Brazier

They are such excellent time keepers and at 4-30.each day stare me out
awaiting their walk.

An Unexpected Caller

Sir Robin Redbreast visited today
He was so beautiful I wished he'd stay
He perching high, looked so disconsolate
Signed sadly to me that he could not wait
He pointed out to me the world he sings
And, Oh, the feel of wind beneath his wings
His world was there, and beautiful, alas
Some unseen barrier he could not pass

He should be free, that I could not deny
His world must be unceilinged, he must fly
I bade him worry not and slowly moved
Up to the window. Seeing he approved
Opened up the casements and said goodbye
He chirped and soared into the waiting sky.

Celia Rees

Cuckoo

Remind me- does the cuckoo
revisit that long field beside the railway line?
Does its note ring through that straggly copse,
No more than forty trees at most?
Where every year, and always on this day
We'd come to listen and be refreshed.

I know that nothing's as it was.
No trains there now. No evening carriages,
Lit like a technicolour film, rushing
From one strange city to another.
And no stroll home, arms linked fast together,
Close as twins, with senses overflowing-yet

I live in hope to hear the cuckoo call
And bring those summers with her in her throat.

Peter Holliday

Reflections of a Dragonfly

My God. I'm just so beautiful,
Just take a look at me.
My wings are so transparent,
And they allow me to be free.

I've spent so long just waiting,
For this moment to arrive.
My metamorphosis was amazing,
And it's wonderful to feel so alive.

I've spent so long under water,
As a nymph and I know it's true.
My adult life is limited,
Need to decide, what am I going to do?

I've only got a few weeks,
To live upon the wing.
I've got to make the most of it
And live life with some Zing.

I'm agile and manoeuvrable,
Can hover and can glide.
Fly forwards and fly backwards,
And sideways....with some pride.

I can rapidly change direction,
And my speed of flight,
But I'm waiting for my mate,
With whom I can unite.

So here I am just waiting,
Sitting out the rain,
The weather has been so awful,
So here I will remain.

My reflection, my reflection
So beautiful can you see?
A wonderful construction of nature.
And My God, It's really me!

Kate Warren   16.6.16

Ornamental Glass Fish
From the perspective of fish.

I am sitting in the window of a charity shop.
The sun is shining in, glinting off my shiny blue fins.
Passers-by glance in at me.
Will they come in and buy me?
Or will they just fondle me?

I dream of being a live fish, swimming in warm, deep seas, dark water
illuminated by gleaming moving corals and the glint of beautiful fish
and sea horses swimming by.
And then?
Would I grow big?
Be caught in the suffocating nets of fishermen?
Be transported to the slab of a fish monger?
Or go directly to a fancy restaurant?
When I'm hot, having been grilled and about to be eaten, will my
secret be discovered?
I have a pearl! It's small and shiny but not completely round.It's
creamy hardness nestling in my soft inside.
Will I be discarded once my secret is out?
Either way my end looms.

Someone is approaching! They pick me up and take me to the till.

Is this the end?

Ronith Bhunnoo

HISTORICAL

The wonder in a child's eyes

It's our wild oceans that sculpture our caves and rocky cliffs
That will carry from mountains cargoes to the flimsy Chinese skiffs.
No longer these fearsome seas are boundaries to mankind
Man's thirst for knowledge pushes him on, new far-off lands to find.

From the frozen Arctic waste where the silver arctic fox can live
To the palm-strewn tropical islands, to see what they have to give.
The tropical fruits, silks and spices from warmer climes
Were brought to our little island home in bygone times

By brave seafarers in fast tall ships by wind and sails
Through angry seas, calm seas and inky black gales,
The silent moon controls their ebb and flow
The stars provide the beacons to guide the mariners where to go.

In times past our enemies have tried to steal the freedom of our island home
But we smashed their ships, and with their blood tinted the British foam
Lord Nelson from his lofty plinth scans London with his sightless eye,
As on gentle breezes clouds from lands he knew so well go drifting by.

Now in this modern age of boats, planes, trains and the family car
Are all part of family life, where sun-warmed sands of distant lands are not so
very far.
The miles of golden sands that hem our pleasant land are a playground for
the masses
Bus-loads of "mums, dads" boys and girls, lads and lassies flock from our
heartland
To be caressed by the breezes of the sea.

Wherever I may wander, wherever I may be, I will forever remember the
Wonder in my child's eye when first he saw the sea.

Denis R.H. Teal   March 2016

The Missing of the Somme

So many fallen faces,
Looking back at me.
Behind their eyes, their feelings
For comrades and family.

Where would their regiment take them?
What battles would they endure?
What did the future hold for them?
What exactly lay in store?

The mud, the blood, the tyranny
Of life hiding in a trench.
The shell- shock, the dysentry,
The trench foot and the stench.

They lived in the ground like rats,
Bombed, gassed and straffed.
They didn't know from day to day,
Which would be their last.

They gave their all, their lives
So we could all be free
From dictatorship and oppression
And live in Democracy.

The treaties, the assassination,
Of one man and his wife,
One million dead, wounded or missing
A catastrophe of life.

Kate Warren

His Story

Once upon a time, children,
One hundred years ago
There was a very bloody war–
Great great grandpa had to go.

Be over in six months, they said
Go out and do your best
For King and Country, then return
A medal on your chest.

We went in droves, few came back whole
What happened in between
The slaughter of the innocents
By the military machine..

I mean both sides. The enemy
Were closer to my mates
Than the fools who gave the orders
And sealed our mutual fates.

When it was finally over
In village, town and city
Names on a peace memorial
Were recalled in pity.

Now the centenary arrives
Surely they wouldn't try
To make it a celebration
Of national victory.

A proper commemoration
For those who gave their life
Would require a resolution:
Non-violent resolving of strife.

Great-great grandchild, I wish for you
A better world than mine
Where nations renounce state violence
And we celebrate mankind.

Charles Eden

THE STORM IS OVER

A lonely gull in a flooded field
Surveying the scar of a storm that's not healed.
The darkened trees in mourning stand
as the raging floods intern the land.
Down from the hills the waters race,
The hungry wind bites the face.
The maiden saplings bow down low
As if to pay homage to the great king blow.
When the storm is over and the scar is healed
Cows will lazily graze in that riverside field.
The now leafless trees will offer shade to the weary
And the thought of the floods will be a memory dreary.
The grass will shoot green
The flood will become a stream.
The thrush will its golden song sing.
From the village church the bells will ring
As memory will fade
To a gone decade.

Denis R.H. Teal

CLENCHER'S MILL, EASTNOR

Last of three
The flour mill sleeps
With eight legged makers
Of lace, groaning with dust
The millwright, keeper of millpick
Releases penstock, gathered nature strength.
The dark, dank, contained watershed
Breathes life and movement into buildings' bones.

Diamonds, glass slivers of light
Pierce the darkness
Connecting the turning, the grinding, the lifting, the heaving.

Masterman, journeyman, apprentice,
Masterman, journeyman, apprentice,
Together in perfectly judged harmony,
Circular, recreating.

The millwright, keeper of millpick
Adjusting the damsel to contain her chattering,
Resisting the blocking, assisting the flow and procedure,
The grain dripping through.

Interconnected, each helping the other,
Vibration and tension,
Relationships, hour upon hour.

The millwright, keeper of millppick
Fills bags of life- for life.
Bags breathe with the life-blood

As lungs, filled to bursting,
Are the start of the new.

Maggie McGladdery
This poem was written in response to a guided tour of the mill.

How Can We Get It So Wrong?

It is said the earth is warming and the ice cap is set to go.
The ozone layer is thinning, there will be less ice and snow.
Our food must be gathered near to hand and produced as nature intended
The hauling fuel from far off lands surely must be ended.
Did we have it so wrong only half a lifetime ago
When every small holding produced milk and butter from the friendly
house cow.
The fuel for my cooker is piped all the way from Russia.
And the chicken in the oven could come from Hong Kong.
How can we get it so wrong?
When I was a lad, now old that I am, all the gas for Bromyard
Came from Bill Morris's and we pushed coke home in a pram.
When we used the switch in the kitchen the lamp would flicker a bit
Then stop.
Cos the electric for Bromyard came from a generator behind Pettifers' shop.
And the water for the Town came from Buckenhill springs,
With the aid of pipes, pumps and tubes, and an old man in a cap, that made
Sure that pure spring water reached every cold tap.
Did we get it so wrong?

Denis R.H. Teal

EVACUEE: MOTHER AND CHILD

I never realised
Until recently
That I too
Was an evacuee.

Born on 1ˢᵗ, August '39
Everyone expecting the worst
Mum and I to her parents flee.
The start of my memory.

I have always wished
I had been born in Devon
To me the county
That is heaven.

Dad was away
With the regiment.
The grandparents ran a school.
At the start and end of every day
Staff and pupils gathered to pray.

A slipway at the harbour
The only place to paddle.
Americans in "Duks" threw us sweets.
At six p.m. everyone gathered in the kitchen
To hear the day's news.

We had a telephone, tall and black.
Vital news came by telegram.
Sitting in my canvas swing one day

My mother snatched me out
A German plane was about.

A house was bombed
A miss-hit for the railway line.
I remember the awe of passing the guns of
The defended Teignmouth bridge.
It served its purpose.
This time!

For my mother to come home
From India, to have me,
To leave a London flat,
Her husband far off,
I was not aware of stress.
I was a fortunate evacuee!

Bryony Cullum   October 2019

LOCKDOWN

VOICES – DURING THE VIRUS

Children laughing
A joy to hear them play
In the sun outside-
I am shut away.

A blackbird with its beak full
Hops onto my wall,
Managing to sing
It pecks up even more!

Was it singing to its wife
Sitting on their nest?
"What did you say you wanted?
I've really done my best."

I hear my neighbour chatting
It must be on her phone.
There are shouts from passers-by.
So much friendliness has grown.

Now voices right across the world,
Emails, conferences, zoom,
I'm not really shut away,
But touch can't come too soon!

Thalia Gordon Clark

Lockdown Blues Away

Within doors almost too tidy
To be called home,
Minute by minute, hour by hour
Days come and go
Unnamed and unremarkable.

Time passes
Nothing
Changes
The sun shines and life stirs.
From the brown earth
Spears come slowly peeping through
The icy ground.
They razor through the silent earth.

Time moves
Something
Changes

Spears surge yearning towards the light.
They are no threat
But the first steps of beauty's feet.
Unfurling slow
Snow drops peep forth so warmly white.

Time sings
Life stirs
Strongly

Warm whiteness daunts the snow and ice.
Crocuses bloom
In white and yellow, purple too
Hellebores glow
Pink with delight among the rest.

Time dances
all things
Are well.

Breath of sweet wind and buds do stir
Promise of glory.
Seeds sown with love rest in the earth
Awaiting warmth
Till they too dance the time away.

Celia Rees

All Change Here!
(in the time of the virus)

We are having to be different.
The "who" we thought we knew,
The one who made decisions,
Has disappeared from view.

The one who knocked on doors,
"How can I help today?"
Now confined in my own house,
Can't help in any way!

My shopping all done for me.
I'll eat what they can find.
"Ah, some of those you've got me.
Thank you- never mind."

I watch the garden flowers,
Yellow, pink and blue,

blossoming so cheerfully
as if they never knew.

All the changes happening,
Changing every day.
I'll be rooted in my garden
Finding sanity that way.

Thalia Gordon Clark

Spring 2021

Sunrays radiate with promise of warmer days.
The winter past stole many lives.
Sanity must prevail.
Cannot go "off the rail".

Keeping busy in solitude.
Radio plays but could not compensate.
The need for a smile, a touch, a hug, a hand to hold
Hope renews with every passing day.
Maybe soon we will be able to visit with family, a friend.
Spring will bring hope.

Rosemary Powell

Thinking Positive

I've always been positive
In my thinking day to day.
So silly being negative,
Your energy drains away.

Think positive - spring is coming soon,
Lighter days and warmer.
I shan't have to keep indoors
And I will feel much calmer.

Then I did a flow test,
As usual I felt positive,
So when the negative answer came
I didn't know what to make of it.

Everyone had been pleased for me,
Said negative is good news,
But when I found I was positive
Everyone changed their views!

Thalia Gordon Clark

Hope

I hope the children come back to the park,
The roundabout, swings and the slide.
The silence, the stillness and ghosts of kids' squeals
Disturb as I pass by outside.

I remember the climbing, the pushing and shouting.
How much I learned as a nipper-
Dynamics of movement and friendships I made.
Somehow it was all so much better.

I hope the children come back to the park;
Leave their screens for the screams of delight
They can have with the physical movement
Of swings as they fly to great heights.

I walk past the quiet
And continue my walk,
Imagining how things might change
If the children return, to stretch their potential,
Turn over a new playful page.

Maggie McGladdery

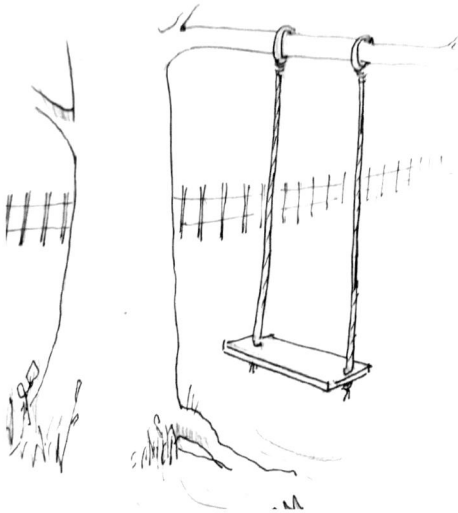

HUMOUR

My Black Hole

There is a greedy black hole in my house
And puppy-like it follows me around.
It may be small but has great gravity
Pulls to itself those items I most need.
Things I lay aside momentarily
To use again right soon are swept away
Lost in its deep, unfathomable dark
Forks, trowels, spoons, scissors and needles too.

Most black holes keep what they take to themselves
Holding it for ever, never seen again,
This one is mischievous, a wicked imp,
What is gone suddenly appears again,
Quite somewhere else, where I have never been,
And where I've looked at least a hundred times.
He's quite capricious as he comes and goes
And hides things in peculiar places.
For I would never, ever put the phone
Out on the fence, or even in the fridge,
Nor yet the scissors in the laundry bag.
Searching for the words he's taken off my tongue,
Losing the shopping list on my way out,
I'm far too sensible for things like that
Eccentric, strange, peculiar, bizarre
That's him not me, of that you may be sure.

Celia Rees

Mockracy

Yes, be a chum to the scum
So that we can
Bash down better
Drill down deeper
Smash down smaller,

First give 'em the old thumbs up
We're mates, don't ever forget
Then into the dressing-up box.
Plenty of japes and jokes galore
So plenty of photo-ops.

We're levelling up, aren't we Dom? Er, Dom?
We'll build back better, I swear
We're blaming the E.U. for our Brexit
And our higher jab rate's only fair.

Get that flag on the building- or else.
Brits are great with their backs to the wall
Traitors alone will still resist it.
Confrontations? We'll win 'em all!

Get the job done. Do it quickly.
They like to see a bit of speed.
Fuck the moaners and their allies,
Fuck the needy – feed the greed.

All right 'we' means 'I', you've got it.
Don't be a dork, it's rhetoric.
Biggest joke in all this circus
Is that they'll still vote for us.

Charles Eden

Eye wear

I wear red,
I wear blue,
I wear purple in several hues,
But my eyes let me down
In this visual game.
How I look, how I seem
How the world is framed.

My wardrobe of rainbows,
And fashion accessories,
I paint on myself and my face,
Self esteem told me to
All those years ago
But now failure is used for success.

Things change, so do I,
Body crumbling and loose
But opportunity beckons,
New presentation in seconds, and
I wear (proudly) the eye wear I choose!

Maggie McGladdery

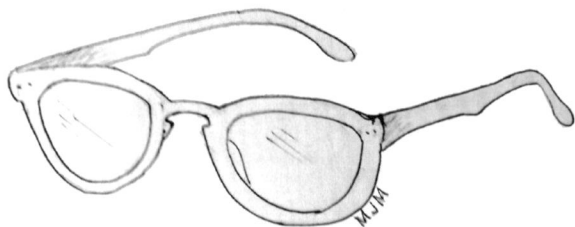

Whoa, Man!

Men enjoy bars
Driving fast cars
Declaring Wars
Paying for whores
Having no cares
Threatening stares
Answering dares
Throwing downstairs
Ignoring laws
Kicking down doors
Avoiding the chores
Befriending bores
Pointing out flaws
Of disputes the cause
Sharpening their claws
Sinking their pars
Having their jars
Thinking they're stars
Men are from Mars

Woman replies
Yeah, whatever......

Charles Eden

The Right Hat

Wearing the right hat
Is important.
I need one for this heat.
Crazy not to have one.

I've lots.
A wife hat,
A mother hat.
A chaplain hat.

Hats for roles
Not for identity.
I don't have a hat
For searching,
Though it's crazy
Searching in the midday sun.

When I've taken off
All my hats
Then I'm searching.

Some people have a listening hat.
I've got one.

You feel you know
who you are
with a hat on.

Crazy
Without a hat
In this heat.

Thalia Gordon Clark

Plucky Pensioner

Plucky Pensioner (66) Protests Press Prejudice
In an unprecedented protest
Plucky Pensioner Percy Pumpkin (66)
Has challenged news-room policies.

Clearly cloyed by clichéd depictions
Of people of pensionable age,
Mr Pumpkin (66) has posed the question
Why mention pensioners in the first place
And why put their age after their name?

Tired of playing the colourful clown
Local personality Pumpkin (66)
Asks if an ageist policy
Is permitted, even promoted.
In press-rooms up and down the country.

Prejudice against older people
Is prohibited in the penal code
And panders to a patronising
Predisposition in most people.

Praise for the important point you raise
You've posed us a puzzler, Percy (66).

Charles Eden

Abode

A little ditty,
An attempt to be witty!
An ode to our new abode.
From Kent to Herefordshire we roamed
With Worcestershire nearby.
Oh my! What wonderful scenic places.

From Snodland to Snodbury,
What a musical Snodfest!

From Womenswold to White Ladies Ashton,
Very caring in Barming, how charming.

From Stoke to Stoke Bliss, who can resist?
From Maidstone to Tedstone,
Partake of a Wafre.
We hailed from Allhallows and aimed for the rolling hills of the
Golden Valley,
With our eye on picturesque Peartree Green,
We milled about at Clenchers
And went from
Paddlesworth to Pudleston,
Just missing North Piddle!

Well Peopleton, my Inkberrow runs dry,
As I'm hoping I'll know Didley squat,
At a Danton Pinch,
About being Postling to the Burley Gate
Of our glorious Sunset years.

Ronith Bhunnoo   2021

NATURE

The Love of Trees

The slender ash, the sturdy oak stand like steeples within
The English hedgerows.
The beech, the birch and the hawthorn are of a gregarious nature
And need the company of a grove to thrive and grow.
The hazel and the sally are viral fellows and will thrive wherever
Nature in her wisdom sought them to sow.
While the tall scotch pine is the guardian of every
Country churchyard.
And the once famous English yew is now just grown
To shade the loo.
The ash makes handles for the woodman's axe,
Chisels, hammers and his trusty spade.
The oak makes tables, church pews and caskets to embrace
Kings when to rest they are laid.
The beech makes our furniture, birch our brooms, hawthorn supports
Our hedges and warms our rooms.
Thank God for our eyes that we may see
The beauty of a living tree.

Denis R.H. Teal

The Raindrop

Every little raindrop holds a world.
A world of wonder and fragility,
A ray of sun gives it a rainbow glow,
Light and airy, a small child's paradise
In which she rounds the world, so beautiful
A bubble of time that holds eternity.

In such a world her eyes can dream the day,
No finger touch for all they long to hold.
Nothing to hear though symphonies unfold.
No smell though freshness fills her aching heart.
No taste though new life tides in her with joy
But mostly fragile love, only, is the way.

Celia Rees

My Garden

The rain,
Oh the rain!
Nourishing, reviving, sustaining
My view.
Those sweet drops of sky nectar,
Descending and soaking
The dryness, the parchedness,
And swelling the bud.

The filling of bucket, of trough
And of can,
Dripping with goodness-
Life diamonds for all.

Maggie McGladdery

Angels

Curling toes in cool scented grass,
Sun on my neck,
Warming like childhood dreams,
Fragrance of honey-coloured honeysuckle
....drifting by.....
Honey bees buzzing, humming a lullaby.

Drowsy, blousy, butterflies hugging

Purple buddleias, preening wings,
Fully stretched showing their beautiful
colours,
Fluttering, dancing in the breeze
As a song thrush starts singing...
... Singing, singing......
Intoxicated by the sweetness of summer.

A sudden whoosh as angels
Glide above the tall silver birches,
Making them rustle and sway.....
On they go.......
Undulating down the valley,
Every thing rippling as they pass.

I believe in angels.....

Looking over towards the Malvern Hills
Dark rain clouds are gathering.
A little rabbit delicately nibbling grass
Looks into my soul with velvet eyes
Before disappearing down his burrow,
White tail bobbing.

Just like Alice in Wonderland
I wonder what happens next
As down the rabbit hole
I go......

Jane Dallow   2014

113

The Whispering Breeze

If when you wander along a woodland way
On a balmy evening after a summer's day
You may hear the evening breeze
Whispering to the stately trees
The pillars of the dying sun
Is a sign to the forest creatures that day is done.
All the life on the woodland floor
Seek shelter for the night once more.
Roosting high the rook and crow
And back to the hive the bees will go.
From the sky the sun sinks down.
Now the woods are filled with an eerie sound.
Now the moon paints a different picture on the page
As the nocturnal actors take the stage.
The fox, the badger, the mouse and rat,
The owl, the nightingale and the pipistrelle bat.
When dawn breaks blood has been spilled.
Death's been quick and hunger fulfilled.
And then begins another day,
Maybe I will see you on that woodland way.

Denis R.H. Teal   2016

MISCELLANEOUS

The Obverse of Time

Time flies say many men.
And man is a slave to time.
Time is no servant to men.
In his home the old man
Has no clock.
On his wrist he has no watch.
You are timeless!
Why don't you have a watch
Or a clock
Asks the visitor.

I don't need them
Came the reply
In a defiant tone.
I have my friend the time
He accompanies me wherever I go.

He takes me everywhere he goes
He is my trusted loyal friend
He is the only one that never let me down.
In time of my trouble.

Nothing soothes me the most
As my friend of eternal
By his silent presence
Of just being
Which wraps all around me
Like a soft warm blanket
And tenderly and lovingly

Like a mother's embrace
To her hurting child.

Like the mother
Time is never in haste.
To eternity forever it flows.
And forever patient.
I float with him to the ether
And he always brings me back in time.

Yet still it stands
But motionless it is not.
It is as timeless as ever.

This is the joy of time,
Who needs a clock!

Zia Bhunnoo   23 12 2021

Lots of Questions

What is home?
Where is home?
When do we begin to call a building home?
How do we find a new home?
When do our feelings cry for home?

Judy Malet

Feathers

When do feathers first fly,
And why?
When did the first bird go up in the sky,
Or did it run like an ostrich for fun?

When did humans first pluck their way
To skin and bone to eat the next day?
Then we filled pillows to keep warm and cosy;
Then dressed up our hats
And got glamorous and posy.
Then men dressed from top to toe
And strutted like a peacock
With an arrow and a bow.

Val Brazier

Ode to Email

Oh! Square window into space.
Fingers capture words.
Then they secretly
Disappear to you.

Judy Malet

A Reflection on Windows

Ever spent time in a hospital ward?
Nothing to look at, totally bored,
Bored too this summer, alone at home,
Curtains still pulled at ten in the morn,
No chance to see dusk or dawn,
Prisoners and patients, one accord.

In a queue one day
Overheard a woman say,
She rejoiced on looking out at each fresh day.
Whatever the weather
Whether or not the weather was OK,
Her life was hers to live her way,
To rejoice in the changes of British Weather.

Poky windows, shut up windows,
Dirty, smeared, or barred up windows,
Some deliberately high
That child, workforce, or captive
Were not allowed to watch what unfurled
In the outside world.

Sash windows, lattice windows,
Dormer, attic, sky-light, bow,
Give style to where they are.
Modern, huge glass edifices,
So hot, so cold inside,
One shudders at the footprint implications,
Clear lifts displaying all, within, without.
Different from checking your image in the shop front!

Those boarded windows in the High Street,
Or in the tenements supposedly out of use,
Tell of times when pride's been beat,
The refuge now a place of refuse.

There are the neighbourhood watch brigade,
Official surveillance,
Or the nosy twitcher behind the lace curtain.
Some employ goggles or sunglasses,
Both shield and distance observer's glances,
Masking the importance of seeing the soul behind.
Eyes, so important, personal windows,
Revealing thoughts, emotions, life.

Bryony Cullum
This poem originated from sharing the hopeless despair of
a very disabled, house-bound friend.

Grow up with hope

Hope wends its way through your life.
Hope to begin to walk.
Hope to learn words to say.
Hope brings the magic of colours.
Hope finds stories to listen to.
Hope brings friends and playgrounds.
Hope begins to show a big world full of discoveries and adventures.

Val Brazier

Angel

I thought I saw an angel
Waiting in the wings
I thought I saw an Angel
With shining silver wings.

I thought I saw an Angel in
Green pastures by the stream
I thought I saw an Angel by
Still waters running deep.

I thought I saw an Angel in the
Valley where dark shadows went before
Until the shadows lifted and the
Light came flooding in and I
Was walking in the air

I thought I saw an angel.

Jane Dallow   2020

A Night Prayer

Out, out sweet candle bear away
The woes and currents of this day,
But leave me still the better part
The love and laughter on the way.

Let not my night be overdone
With nightmares which are not much fun.
Leave fears and worries far behind
And let my dreams of peace be spun.

Give me a deep refreshing sleep;
My o'er stretched mind in safety keep.
Strengthen me for another day
Of ways both beautiful and steep.

Celia Rees

CAPITAL

Received economic opinion says
That London is the main generator
Of wealth, even work, that benefits us all
So don't be a success denigrator.

You don't like our skyline and what it stands for?
It's just a self-confident world city
The envy of many - some would say all.
Steel and glass isn't going to be pretty.

So all right, St. Paul's is a little bit lost
Down below amongst skyscraper shadows
Building always means winners and losers,
Ignore all those nostalgic saddos.

You say there are oligarchs hiding their loot
Helped by lawyers, banks, and their cronies,
You'll quickly discover the law's on our side
And that all your charges are phoney.

Less of a dynamo, more of a cancer?
Now you have taken leave of your senses
Get out of town by the shortest of routes
Before you commit more offences.

Yes, crawl back to your shires and grim northern towns.
You sad chavs who share this gross view
And patiently wait for the wealth to seep down
Hee haw ho! What prize chumps! Toodle-oo!

Charles Eden

My Favourite Hobby

It could be poetry or reading, walking or swimming, tapestry or talking,
But gardening comes to the fore, it has so many facets.
"And in my hand a forest lies asleep." Quote from The Seed Shop, a
favourite poem.
Perhaps the best of gardening is for me the vision of what might become.
Every shopping excursion passes a favourite source
Never mind markets and garden centres enticing a buy.
Gardening, so many aspects! Appearance, physical effort, fresh air,
Edible produce, flowers for arrangements, rejuvenating space.

Wildlife provides surprises; a barn owl gliding just overhead, frogs and
toads jump and scuttle,
A spade reveals a nestled newt, a swarm of bees zoom round a corner.
Birds. Integral. Songs of blackbird, thrush and robin, dunnocks rustling in
the hedge,
Tits and finches at their feeding stations, jackdaws on the roof.

Foliage! There's a thought, a single grass, a glossy bough,
Palmate fronds, clustered leaves or jagged spikes form pictures.
Think of colours; myriads of leafy greens, multitudinous, vivid or pastel
shaded flowers.
A single bloom, a posy, a border, plants of all shapes and sizes making a
statement for insects and us.

Seasonal? Yes, indeed, but then there are books. I love The Morville
Hours,
The works of personalities, both authors and TV stars; catalogues and
magazines
Others' gardens absorb attention.
Delights of seasons themselves visible and felt from inside or without.
Smells, cut grass, blossom, blooms, fruit or scented bowers.

So I dig, weed, plant and prune, manure and water,
Tie a tether, tend and transplant, compost and burn
Muscles of arms, legs, stomach, back have their turn
As I indulge in my favourite hobby, gardening.

Bryony Cullum   29/09/2010

A world to look forward to

I'm looking forward to the rising temperatures,
A world on fire while we turn a blind eye.
Carbon emissions, a smothering blanket of smog.
The climate crisis like a time bomb,
The seconds tick, tick, ticking away.

I'm looking forwards to the white supremacy.
Our "superior race" that can't tolerate others,
A black man is killed on the streets by the hands of a supposed
"saviour."
Whilst the justice system started to build his defence.
How is abuse and hate normality?

I'm looking forwards to the incompetence of governments,
Those useless leaders,
Bumbling idiots bringing a country to its knees,
Always the first to blame another,
Saving themselves as we're left to sink.

I'm looking forwards to the climbing prices.
The poor getting poorer: the rich getting richer
Unable to afford the cost of living,
With no one to respond to the frantic SOS calls,
Living in poverty and hell on earth.

I'm looking forwards to getting cat-called in the street,
Told to "Give us a smile" or how to dress.
My body, my choice, until it's not –

Don't call the police, flag down a bus!
Why? Because it turns out the monsters wear a uniform too.

A life of fear, a world of hate,
That's what I'm looking forwards to.

Meg

Cloud Shapes

There's a pale wind blowing
The sky is winter blue
With the sun shining through
A multitude of clouds,
Turning them every colour
From golden yellow,
Darkest pink to pale candyfloss bubbles.
Oh,what pictures of delight
Float before our eyes.

There's a map of dear old England
With a little puff
Of Ireland by the side.
Dolphins racing
On a choppy sea of blue
And on the tallest mountain summits
Are giant birds,
Their wings tinged with orange,
Blue and sandy brown.

A school of big white whales
All blowing through their airways,
Chased by giant whalers in full sail.
An elephant at sea meets them
Head on at speed.
They nod to one another
Before disappearing toute suite.

Dainty flowers... whole rose bowers,
The horizon lit up like the Champs Elysees
Without a Frenchman in sight,
But a troupe of can-can dancers
In skirts of many colours
Stretch across the sky.

Black velvet night
With the stars shining bright
And the moon as its light.
Wispy clouds floating by
Catching sight of the man in the moon.

Jane Dallow   2013

My Treasure Chest

We are but tiny creatures upon this great big earth
A lifetime is but a day to the gigantic universe.
Yet still we worry, strain and stress
To gather the trinkets of earthly gain.

But I've found the secret within life's span
Is to collect the things that make the man.
For pleasure I get from a golden sunset
And joy at the sight of a swallow in flight
These gains I bank with meticulous care
And store them with dreams and thoughts that are rare.
When my life is ending and dusk is drawing near
The treasures which I've gathered will help me stem the fear
For then will I remember the smile of a newborn babe
Which will help me travel that lonely road to the grave.

Denis R.H. Teale

Denis Teal

We mourn the passing of Denis. He was an early member of the group and whole-heartedly supported the various activities in which we have engaged: from our monthly meetings at The Falcon, regular visits to care homes, supporting the Children's Poetry Competition and responding to local events. His photographic contributions are lovely mementos.

Denis was an encyclopaedia of matters Bromyard and a wonderful story teller. In his poetry he expressed his love of nature and animals as well as reflecting on serious events and his personal philosophy. He was such a kind and sensible man. We always looked forward to his readings. He is sadly missed.

ABOUT THE POETS

Ronith Bhunnoo. I've enjoyed reading and writing poetry since childhood and still find it to be my release for expressing all emotions.

I've engendered an appreciation of poetry in my previous learners, whether it be Shakespeare or rap and shared poems with my family, friends and colleagues.

Zia Bhunnoo. A new member to our group.

Val Brazier. I have lived in Bromyard for over forty years and am a very recent member of the Poetry Group. A retired teacher and having written many stories for children over the years , I find the sidestep I have made into the genre of reading and writing poetry both stimulating and interesting.

Bryony Cullum. Originally just a reader and listener, my involvement has evolved into sharing poetry with young and old as well as those in between.

Jane Dallow. I enjoy poetry and over recent years have taken to expressing some of my thoughts and feelings by writing my own. I was born in Herefordshire and have lived here all my life. I was lucky to marry a Herefordshire man and to have 2 daughters. Without the support and encouragement of the Bromyard poetry group I doubt whether I should have become involved with poetry.

Charles Eden. For me poetry is the natural way of celebrating the personal. The most significant moments are to do with being present in the present, present in the here and now.

Thalia Gordon Clark. I was introduced to poetry at home and through education.

It has been a continual element in my life. Poems learnt by heart have remained to use whenever the occasion arises.

Graham Hamblin. 83, has lived in Bromyard for 13 years, after spending the previous 20 years as a bookseller in Exeter. Favourite poet Philip Larkin.

Peter Holliday. I was born in Hereford and have lived in Welsh Border Country for almost 50 years. I was Leominster's Librarian for more than 20 years. I lecture widely on local history. I strive to write good poetry with the star of Seamus Heaney before me.

Judy Malet. Having lived in England, Scotland, India and Africa, I have always wanted to "belong" somewhere. Herefordshire has given me that wish and the time to write thoughts in poems.

Maggie McGladdery. Since retiring I have returned to painting but I am also enjoying my discovery of painting with words.

Rosemarie Powell.
Born and raised in rural Herefordshire
Spread wings into city life.
Strove for gold in Africa,
Freedom and challenge in America.
Full circle to enjoy the "quiet" life.
Encouraged by family and friends, began a new adventure with poetry back in Herefordshire.

Celia Rees. I often find that by reading poetry that poets have put into words thoughts and feelings I have been trying to express. It is a relief to listen or read about scenes and stories outside the present.

Denis, R.H. Teal. I was born at Kyrebach, Thornbury. On leaving school at 15, I became a van boy for Goldings' hardware. I trained as a medic in the R.A.F. for my National Service. Married with 4 children, I managed the largest supermarket in Herefordshire, at the time, but left to work less hours at a pet shop in Worcester until 1998, when I retired and became photographer for the Bromyard Gala and Off the Record. In spite of my meagre education I enjoy poetry and have written some poems.

Kate Warren. I was very fortunate to have an inspiring primary school teacher who instilled in me a love of poetry.

Robin Wilson. I am seriously dyslexic and struggle to read or write but words and ideas flow through me and I enjoy putting them down.

ILLUSTRATIONS/ART WORK by

INDEX OF POETS